NNSYLVANIA

Greetings from Pottstown

Patricia Wanger Smith

Schiffer Publishing Ltd®
4880 Lower Valley Road, Atglen, Pennsylvania 19310

Acknowledgments

A deep debt of gratitude is owed to the photographers of yore such as E. D. Miller, Eugene Orlando, and the many unsung and unnamed people who made this book possible by their contributions to the preservation of our history through their pictorial efforts. Many historians have contributed much to the saving of our history in writing. Among these to be lauded are Chancellor & Wendell for their book *History of Pottstown 1752-1952*, Edmunds Claussen for his several histories of the area, and Estelle Cremers for her book, *Coventry, The Skool Kill District*. Much of the material used in this book has come from the collection of Charles Moyer, a longtime friend. Without these literary folks, photographers, and collectors; Kathryn Ballein, my friend with the poised red pen; the editors at Schiffer Publishing, and Schiffer itself for being an interested publisher with many helpful employees; and you, the readers, who may be inspired to bring your collective histories to life while reading, this book could not have been written. It is therefore to you, the reader, to whom this book is dedicated.

Other Schiffer Books on Related Subjects
The Brandywine, 0-916838-06-4, $12.95
Ghosts of Valley Forge and Phoenixville, 978-0-7643-2633-2, $14.95
West Chester: A Review in Early Postcards, 978-0-7643-2707-0, $29.95

Library of Congress Control Number: 2008925240

Designed by Mark David Bowyer
Type set in Grouch BT / Souvenir Lt BT

ISBN: 978-0-7643-2986-9
Printed in China

Published by Schiffer Publishing Ltd.
4880 Lower Valley Road
Atglen, PA 19310
Phone: (610) 593-1777; Fax: (610) 593-2002
E-mail: Info@schifferbooks.com

Please visit our web site catalog at **www.schifferbooks.com**

In Europe, Schiffer books are distributed by:
Bushwood Books
6 Marksbury Ave.
Kew Gardens
Surrey TW9 4JF
England
Phone: 44 (0)208 392-8585
Fax: 44 (0)208 392-9876
E-mail: Info@bushwoodbooks.co.uk

Website: www.bushwoodbooks.co.uk
Free postage in the UK. Europe: air mail at cost.
Try your bookstore first.

Contents

Chapter One

Advertising & Postcards

Advertising Cards

Advertising cards have an earlier history than postcards. Their peak was from circa 1876 to 1900. Their true popularity began after the Centennial celebration in Philadelphia in 1876, where attendees were given some of these new color advertising cards extolling tradesmen's wares or services. Victorian trade cards became the Madison Avenue advertising of their time. The cards were readily available to merchants who freely distributed them to prospective and current customers, springing to life whole new markets. Many printers jumped on the bandwagon to produce these colorful items; many salesmen were employed to contact the current merchant customers and to recruit new ones. At home the women and children of the household not only read the blurb about the best of what was being touted by the pictures and words, but many of these families turned the pretty pictures into lovely Victorian scrapbooks that have survived to this day. Not only were words important, but also pictures which in many instances gave the non-literate person a piece of advertising he or she could understand. The blurbs or pictures might have included a puzzle called a rebus; sometimes the card was mechanical, usually showing a complete change in the original picture; and sometimes the card was the shape of the item being advertised. Just as today, beautiful women, sweet little children, and sometimes comedy were used to draw the recipient of the card to the vendor. Television uses these techniques, but leaves us with nothing on which to practice our reading skills or to paste in a picture album. The important thing to remember about advertising cards is that they were the merchant's link to his customers. There was no telephone book. There was no Internet. The only way to encourage new business or retain old customers lay in the use of these delightful, often whimsical or sometimes practical, advertising cards. Incidentally, they remain one of the few bargains left in the world of antiques.

Postcards

Around 1900 the shift in advertising seemed to favor the newly introduced postcard. At the Columbian Exposition in Chicago in 1893 the postal card was introduced. There were two types: the government card had a one-cent post stamp imprinted on it while the souvenir cards required an adhesive two-cent stamp. For the brief period of 1898 to 1901, a private mailing card was printed and sold by printers. These cards bore the inscription of "Private Mailing Card" and required a one-cent stamp. The United States Postal Service granted the use of the word "postcard" in 1901 and the private citizenry began to use black and white photographs printed on card stock to send pictures of themselves, their homes, and other worthwhile scenery to friends and relatives. All this while, the back of the card was blank for the address only. No writing was permitted there, so the users of these cards had to write around, beneath, above the picture or anywhere they could on the front side of the card in order to send a note to the recipient. Today these are referred to as real photos cards and command a higher price than do mass manufactured cards.

In 1907 the divided back card made its debut and folks no longer had to crowd their message on the front with the picture. At this time the German printers and lithographers introduced some of the finest cards ever printed for the U.S. public. This continued until the outbreak of World War I when England and the United States took over this aspect of postcards.

To cut back on the cost of ink, a white border was used in the period covering 1915 to 1930. Many poorer quality cards were made during this time. But, regardless of the quality, many older folks will remember fondly the actual sites of these cards because they were made shortly before or after their birth.

From 1930 until 1944 a process using a high rag content made postcards having a texture to them. These cards are called "linens." Many times they were garishly or unnaturally colored because of the dyes used in their making.

After 1944 Photochromes entered the market with colors true to their natural surroundings. These are the cards of today, produced now by digital cameras and not by film cameras. Cards having an age greater than thirty years generally will command more value than newer cards unless there has been a drastic change in the landscape or building. A fire, a natural disaster, or a momentous occurrence, such as the World Trade Center tragedy of 9-11, makes people scurry to get cards of the area prior to its change. This in turn drives up the prices.

Beauty is truly in the eye of the beholder when it comes to postcards. People collect all manner of cards. Some want views of their hometown, which we hope is augmented by this book. Others want railway stations, racecars, courthouses, hospitals, people, no people, airplanes, military bases, hot air balloons, and just about any subject you can imagine. Some want unique advertising cards, which brings this discussion full circle. Yes, there is still advertising being sent on postcards, but somehow the beauty and certainly the quaintness of those early endeavors has been lost. This book incorporates the blending of the two media, postcards and advertising cards, to add more flavor and appeal to the history of Pottstown, the Coventries, and the Pottsgroves.

Chapter Two

Remembering Pottstown

When you 'remember' Pottstown, what does that mean to you, the reader, the purchaser, or the recipient of this book? Is it where you, your parents, grandparents, or great grandparents were born? Did you grow up here? Did you receive your education here? Did you or your parents work here? Perhaps you attended church or synagogue here and were baptized, confirmed, Bar or Bas Mitzphaed, in this town. Were you married here? Were you involved in sports as a participant or a spectator? Did you shop here? Did you swim or dance at Sunnybrook? Were you ever in the hospital here? If any of these scenarios relates to you, then sit back and page through some colorful, historical pictures of places you'll remember or were told about as a child.

Greetings from Pottstown contains not only picture postcards, but some actual photos and copies of advertising used by our merchants to entice our business. As an author, I hope to awaken not only your memories, but perhaps bring to you enough history and lore to kindle your desire to learn more about the Pottstown area and its many gifts to the world. Some of these things may have been before your time, but perhaps you heard the "old timers" talk of them. Perhaps you could invite one of the "old timers" of today to sit with you and add their recollections to these pictures. Perhaps you will look at the remaining architecture of our town in a new light. Check out the hidden facades beneath twentieth century coverings.

Many cards could have been used in this introductory section. This method of messaging loved ones, friends, and acquaintances would seem to surpass the cold, mechanical emails of today. Our children and grandchildren will have nothing to pass on to future generations because all that we write to one another is deleted all too quickly with just one click. Think about it: when was the last time you received a non-business letter?

From 1907, this is our title card. It says it all: Seeing Pottstown, Pennsylvania. Perhaps for many, in reflecting on the past, the town and its surrounding townships will blossom with a new light projected from an older era.

This souvenir card shows a quick overview of our town featuring cards from 1908.

Many people, indeed, did find their love in Pottstown.

Printed in Germany, this souvenir card pictures beautiful ladies from the 1910 era.

Well, if you can't be there, perhaps this book is the next best thing.

Chapter Three

Early Pottstown History

ər an idea, through the use of real photo nd ordinary postcards of Pottstown and of what it was like in the early part of the o start, it has always been said, is at the

Lenape Indians were the first to gather River. Many artifacts, such as arrowheads, ince the 1700s, leading many to believe lace for these early people. The Native nen who dared to traverse the wilderness. se in exchange for needed "modern tools" o such early traders were Pierre Bizaillion idian traders, who plied the waters of the ottstown Landing and Spring City around ıp an outpost trading site near present day wnship. The first actual settlers in the area ir homes along the banks of the Schuylkill ıat they named Morlatton, now Douglass- of Chester County.

ve find that iron ore discovered locally was nd growth of Pottstown and its environs. fty-year-old English Quaker friend of Wil- Rutter took his friend's plea seriously when ablishing a forge, so Rutter ventured some lelphia home to an area just northwest of Hill near Pine Forge, where he built Pool ype forge utilizing a primitive charcoal iron of this first forge in the colony occurred ıny Creek circa 1714-1715. One might say that this was the critical point in the establishment of the "iron" dynasties in this area. Another one was Coventry Forge along the French Creek in Chester County that was built in 1719 by Samuel Savage. Then Thomas Potts joined Thomas Rutter in 1719 in the establishment of Colebrookdale Furnace. Samuel Nutt founded at least four furnaces in the Chester County area including Rock Run Furnace in 1726, Coventry Steel Furnace (the first steel furnace in Pennsylvania) in 1732, the Reading Furnace in 1733, and the Warwick Furnace in 1737. Thomas Potts, Jr. built Mt. Pleasant Furnace in 1737 followed by a forge in 1743. Hopewell Furnace, a National Historic Site in our back yard so to speak, was built by William Byrd in 1743. Why, you might ask, is all this important? Well, all these families inter-married a number of times, the most notable of which, for this undertaking, is the marriage of John Potts, Pottstown's founder, to Ruth Savage, the granddaughter of Thomas Rutter.

Pottstown's history could never be told in detail in a picture book, but the historical highlights of the town will be presented. John Potts, the town's founder, was born in Germantown in 1710. He was a member of the Society of Friends and was educated in Philadelphia. His father, Thomas, was an early iron master who worked with his friend and iron pioneer, Thomas Rutter. Thomas Potts had sons and Thomas Rutter had granddaughters. John and two of his brothers became husbands to these young women. Finding things a bit "crowded in the cabin" with thirteen children, John and his wife decided to build a manor house for their brood. They decided on a site in western Philadelphia County, now of course Montgomery County. Construction of Pottsgrove Manor took two years, beginning in 1752. With its commanding view and closeness to the Great Road, running from Philadelphia to Reading and points west, its use of the finest artisans with the best quality materials, and its décor the most excellent the period had to offer, this home was undeniably the finest seen thus far in this immediate area. It rivaled many of the Philadelphia mansions of its time. Its acreage of nine hundred and ninety five acres was part of New Hanover and Douglass Townships; Pottsgrove Township did not exist.

In 1752 John designed the town of Pottsgrove, the first town in present Montgomery County, bounded by Charlotte Street to the east, York Street to the west, Beech Street to the north, and the Schuylkill River to the south. One hundred feet wide, the High Street he designed is a continued blessing in the twenty-first century with its motorized traffic. The British origins of his family are present in the names of the streets, while the names of trees complete the other streets in the original town design.

Potts appropriated ground for churches. Some, including the Quaker and Reformed congregations, took advantage of this gift early on. Some taverns and inns were present in the town because of the Great Road and its linking of Philadelphia to the western countryside. However, at the time of Potts' death, reports said that there were no more than twelve to fifteen homes, a grain mill in Gabel's field, and a rope tow across the Schuylkill River. John Potts chose to be buried in the family plot, in his beloved town. That plot is on Chestnut Street between Hanover and Penn Streets.

This pin back button shows General St.Clair with all his military finery.

A stylized view of the manor is pictured here. This card dates from 1940 and was written by Marjorie Potts Wendell to Mrs. Leonard Potts thanking her for her assistance in raising money for the manor. The card also affords a nice picture of the caretaker's home.

General George Washington, an acquaintance of John Potts, chose what is now Lower Pottsgrove in which to make his encampment with the struggling Continental Army after their defeat at the Battle of the Brandywine in 1777. Washington marshaled his troops from Pottsgrove to take on the English General Howe at the disastrous Battle of Germantown in a valiant effort to recapture Philadelphia. Thoroughly devastated, the battered troops gathered themselves, their meager supplies, and equipment to spend the now famous winter of 1777 at Valley Forge. Washington made his headquarters in the home of Isaac Potts, John and Ruth Savage Potts' fourth son.

It certainly was not a secret that all those early iron men – the Potts, the Rutters, the Savages, and the Nutts – formed a nucleus of much needed iron supplies for the American Revolution. However, not all the kin in John Potts' family embraced the rebellion. John, Jr. remained a Tory loyal to England, which caused the seizing of his properties when the new government came into power. Major General Arthur St. Clair bought that property at the southeast corner of High and Hanover Streets. Elected from Pottsgrove to serve in the Continental Congress, St. Clair became the newly formed body's first president, its highest office. Some would say he was the first president of our country because of this. Montgomery County, formed in 1784, included Pottsgrove and the surrounding area. Several times during the eighteenth and nineteenth centuries, movements formed to create a new county comprised of western Montgomery, northern Chester, and eastern Berks Counties that would be called St. Clair County, with Pottstown as its county seat.

Known as the Mill Park Hotel for many years, John Potts' beloved Pottsgrove fell into disrepair until its fate was changed by the Pottstown Historical Society who took it up as a cause in the mid twentieth century. Their interest in the restoration of this once fine mansion was instrumental in saving it for future generations. Once administered by the state of Pennsylvania, its operations are now in the care of Montgomery County. The county provides many varied cultural programs throughout the year to appeal to a variety of tastes.

The restored basement kitchen of the old manor home beckons visitors to learn how meals were made and who made them for the Potts clan.

About thirty years ago the manor house looked much like this picture.

Chapter Four

Waterways

The Schuylkill River, named by early Dutch settlers, and the Manatawny Creek, named by the Lenni Lenape and meaning "where we drank liquor," have always been influential in the growth of Pottstown. Waterpower was essential to the early iron forges, many of which were found along the Manatawny. The Schuylkill River and later the Schuylkill Canal, completed in 1821, added much to the economy of the burgeoning town. Coal could be carried from the anthracite-mining region of Pennsylvania to Pottstown and, in fact, to Philadelphia with the advent of the canal. Although the canal ran on the south side, or the Coventry side, of the river, its economic boon to Pottstown is undeniable. The village of Pottstown Landing grew just to service this new industry. This series of cards will acquaint you with those waterways, their bridges, and some of their uses whether they are for work or play.

These gentlemen appear to be decked out in their finest boat wear for rowing on the river. Sailboats on the river seem very unusual today.

This card, possibly from the 1940s, lends an air of serenity to the Schuylkill River.

Just a few miles west of Pottstown stands the 1716 home of Mounce Jones. This was in the first settlement by the Swedes to the area, which they called Morlatton and is now Douglassville.

Although not in the surrounding six townships of Pottstown, this bridge at Douglassville was an important crossing for early residents of the area and its importance to early commerce cannot be discounted.

A latter day color picture finds it just before its demise in the later portion of the twentieth century.

The Hanover Street Bridge was rebuilt a number of times since its early toll paying covered bridge days; this card from the 1920s shows the manner of construction of the bridge at that time. Prior to the building of the Route 100 bypass, this bridge carried the majority of traffic into Pottstown. This view is looking into town.

Looking back at the bridge from the Pottstown side during a flood, possibly in 1938, the Schuylkill is not so tame anymore. Lord's Grocery and the Pennsylvania Railway Station have taken on a lot of water.

The third vehicular bridge across the Schuylkill River at Pottstown is the Kenilworth Bridge. Kenilworth's original name was Madison. This bridge, built in 1868 and destroyed just ten years later in 1878, bears the name of Madison Bridge. The current narrow bridge was built in 1937-1938. This photo was taken in 1870 and the folks pictured seem to be standing on broken ice floes created by the breakup of the river ice.

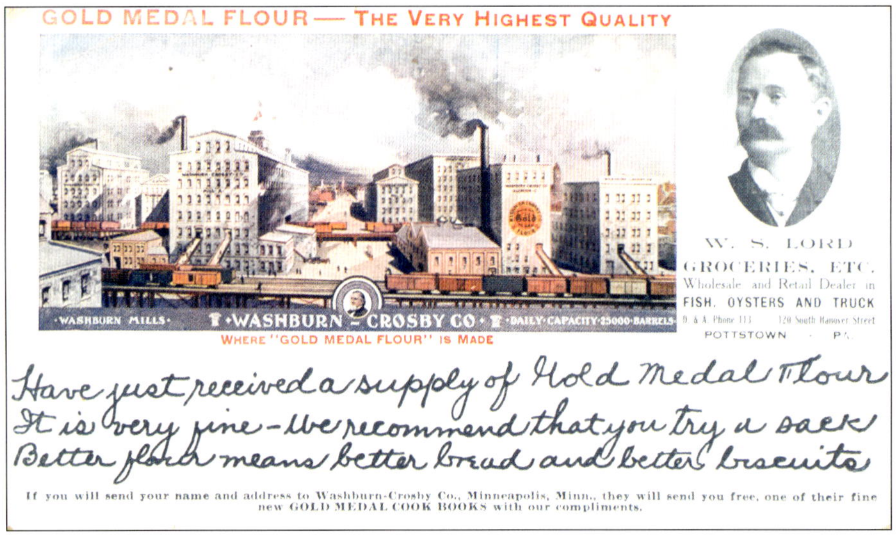

A picture of Mr. Lord appears on this advertising card for his store and Gold Medal Flour.

This was the steel span built in 1882 to replace the covered bridge to Madison.

Another view of the locks shows a closer view of its workings.

In what is now North Coventry Township, then just Coventry Township, the Schuylkill Canal created its own village to meet the wants of its workmen and travelers. Pottstown Landing as it is called was entered on the National Registry of Historic Places just a few years ago to commemorate the fact that it is the only village in the state that was created solely for the purpose of serving the needs of the Schuylkill Canal. There was a veterinarian and a blacksmith for the mules who pulled the barges. There were stores and a bakery for the people to garner supplies. There was a boat builder to build, mend and repair the barges. There was a coal yard to take in the yields from the coalmines up river. All these enterprises led farm acreage to become developed. Sounds familiar, and this was between 1820 and 1850! A fine picture of the Laurel Hill Locks is shown here. It is now on the private property of Laurel Locks Farm.

Canoeing on the Schuylkill Canal about where the Routes 100 and 422 bridges now cross in Pottstown Landing was a pleasant diversion after the canal was no longer needed for the transporting of goods. Saylor's Coal Yard in seen in the background. The canal barges became outfitted as people carriers for picnicking along the canal banks in later years.

This young lady is pictured standing on the bridge seen in the background of a preceding view. Written Saturday morning, she is asking the recipient if she wishes to attend the poultry show or the opera, or both, that evening after they meet at the Ellis Mills Store in Pottstown. This says something about mail service in the good old days of 1906.

South Pottstown has seen its share of Schuylkill River flooding. This picture is from the 1938 flood.

This view portrays the 1902 flooding of the Schuylkill at Pottstown Landing with the Warwick Iron Company seen in the distance.

Coming back across the Hanover Street Bridge, this is a view of the long gone Water Street during the same flood. All the homes were razed along Water Street when it became the site for Industrial Highway.

This picture was taken on Hanover Street, facing the bridge and looking south, showing the flooding generated from Hurricane Agnes in 1972. Lord's Grocery, Jolly's original restaurant, the train station, and even Mrs. Smith's Pies have been long gone from this scene. This is the area currently under development for housing and small businesses.

The exploration of waterways leads us to the Manatawny Creek, which is seen here at the now demolished dam. It offers a view, captured before 1907, of High Street and an open trolley car.

Looking west towards the Manatawny Creek, people are seen rescuing their belongings along King Street during Hurricane Agnes. Some elderly and infirm were taken by rowboats from their homes to above the York Street intersection.

A later view shows the bridge having been replaced with steel and appearing much as it does today. The Pottstown Brewery is seen to the right. A nice old Mail Pouch Tobacco ad graces the rear of the brick building, which is also on the right.

The P & R Railroad Bridge in this vicinity shows rail cars filled with coal from the coal regions to the north. The railway spelled the demise of transport on the Schuylkill Canal. In fact, the railway purchased the canal to insure that rail business transporting this commodity would flourish.

Many of these homes along Manatawny Street and the creek are still there.

This view is looking south on the Manatawny Creek at the King Street Bridge. The icehouse is on the left. Before the advent of home electric refrigeration, ice harvesting was done along such streams. The ice was sold to consumers, usually by home delivery, to use in their iceboxes. Of course, now the iceboxes are valuable collector's items.

Looks like these gentlemen are having a relaxing day fishing along the Manatawny.

Flooding at Manatawny Park next to the creek is an all too frequent occurrence. This flood is from 1915. The writer of the card says that he took the picture with his new camera.

This lovely card was the cover of a solicitation for funding to build the War Memorial Park after World War II in 1946.

Some of the funds collected were used for this playground, pavilion, and wading pool. The pool was free to the general public and a great way to beat the summer's heat.

Chapter Five

Railroads

With the advent of railways, small towns became linked to the larger cities and Pottstown was no exception. In the early to mid twentieth century, people could travel easily from their small towns and villages to places such as Reading and Philadelphia. After the 1960s rail service was limited to hauling commodities in the outlying areas, and only those communities near Philadelphia enjoyed commuter lines.

Perhaps just a few years later, this was the scene at the Reading Railroad Station in Pottstown, coming east from the Stowe Station.

Even Stowe, Pottstown's little neighbor to the west, had its own railway station. This was how it looked in 1913.

This shows the renovation and rebuilding of the station. Although today a bank, it looks much the same.

In this early real photo card we see the rebuilding of railroad track. It is unknown if the construction was the result of an accident or reconstruction to prevent flooding of the rails next to the river.

Just down Hanover Street at the intersection of Water Street, now Industrial Highway, were the Pennsylvania tracks and station shown here.

This view of the "Pennsy" Station shows the Pottstown Roller Mills in the background. Prior to its becoming an apartment complex, the building housed one of the oldest businesses in town. Opened in 1725, the Roller Mills served the farmers in the area for the milling of their grain harvests. In later years, the mill continued the sale of grains, not necessarily milled on site, to provide food for the farmers' animals. Prior to and during WWII flour purchased from the mill came in "fancy" cotton bags from which frugal housewives made clothing and quilts. Vintage material from that era is worth a small fortune today to quilters, and reproductions abound.

Just east of town the trains took the Chester County side of the Schuylkill River, crossing at this site.

Whoops! This unscheduled stop occurred prior to 1915 near Pottstown.

Just east of Pottstown in present-day East Coventry was the whistle stop of Frick's Locks, pictured in this postcard from Mr. Miller's series of cards printed prior to 1915.

Chapter Six

Industries

The iron and steel industry so important to Pottstown's earliest beginnings was in its heyday in the early twentieth century. It remained strong until after the middle of the twentieth century when cheap foreign steel began to flood the markets. There were certainly many more diverse industries present in the area than there are postcards available to portray them.

Shown is the iron mill at Glasgow in a real photo card.

The Potts Brothers' Mill, begun in 1846, is pictured here in 1905. In 1892 it was noted for its manufacture of boiler and tank plates.

This card, printed in Germany, shows the Warwick Furnace in 1908. Every evening at a certain time this furnace dumped the slag it produced that day. It not only lit the countryside, but also served as a clock for local young people to "get on home" as it was 9 p.m.

Eastern Steel Company is pictured here. This card also affords a good view of West High Street, the bridge over the Manatawny Creek, and on the right Pottsgrove Manor, peeping through the trees.

Bramcote, a suburb of Stowe, had a dye works, shown here prior to 1907. The card says dye, but it is felt this should be "die" for die casting, which seems much more plausible for this area.

The Light Manufacturing Company made bicycles, early automobiles, and auto parts and was located south of High Street. During a strike of the workers, detectives escorted "scabs," marked by X's, from Philadelphia so that the company could continued to operate. The card dates from about 1910.

The McClintic-Marshall Company was the forerunner of Bethlehem Steel in the Pottstown community. McClintic-Marshall took over the Philadelphia Bridge Works in 1900. In 1928, McClintic-Marshall also assumed control of the Pottstown Iron Company.

This card circa 1923 depicts two early industries in town — the Hydro United Rubber Company, an early tire maker, and the Glasgow Iron Company.

Bethlehem Steel, their headquarters shown in this card from the 1960s, acquired McClintic-Marshall in 1931; and, finally in 1936 all the shops began to operate under the name of Bethlehem Steel.

For many years the Firestone Tire and Rubber Company flourished in the eastern end of Pottstown. It employed thousands of area men and women after World War II.

Janney & Wickersham produced an electric water level indicator for steam boilers, certainly an important commodity for industry.

The "Low Down" Crown Warm Air Furnace, because of its design, enabled its installation in low ceiling cellar spaces. The March-Brownback Stove Company manufactured these and other models such as the Welcome Globe Range. The stove company moved from their location in Limerick, to South Street between Charlotte and Penn Streets in 1892. At the time of their demise, they were manufacturing castings for the jobbing industry.

The Colebrookdale Foundry, in nearby Douglass Township, Berks County, had its beginnings also tied to the early Rutter enterprises along the Manatawny Creek. Although these two cards picture areas just beyond the stated boundaries established for this book, they are important in telling the story of the iron and steel industry in the area.

The rolling mill at Pine Forge traces its history back to Thomas Rutter. Its claim to fame lay in the manufacturing of a tough steel plate used in construction of locomotives. Virtually the entire village of Pine Forge was tied economically to the mill in years gone by.

An advertisement for the Chadwick automobile offers it to the public for $5,500, certainly a car only for those of means in that era of 1907. Even though the cars were manufactured in Pottstown, Chadwick's main offices were in Philadelphia.

Seen here August 19, 1900, at the Indianapolis Speedway, this Chadwick racer was proclaimed the winner of the Free for All — the fastest stock car in the world!

A 1910 Chadwick Runabout and a 1907 Touring Car are featured in these cards. The autos, taken for testing on local country hill roads, frightened the farm children of the area. The children who had never before seen or heard these noisy contraptions scattered to the safety of the cornfields.

St. Peters also provided granite from its mines. A whole village grew up because of the mining industry in that small area of Chester County. This card is from 1915.

This card, postmarked in 1914, is actually pre 1907. Were these youngsters visiting the Old Charcoal Iron Forge at St. Peters or did they work there? St. Peters is just south of North and South Coventry in Warwick Township.

Although roughly seven miles from Pottstown, the Limerick Nuclear Generating Station and its cooling towers have dominated the Pottstown area for more than twenty five years. Still a large employer, its construction attracted thousands of new workers to the area.

Chapter Seven

Fire Companies

Vital to any community, the volunteer fire companies of Pottstown and its local townships are no exceptions to the rule. They stand ready for all emergencies. Unfortunately, postcards of all of them do not exist in these collections.

This great postcard, from 1906, shows the Philadelphia Steam Fire Company's engine on High Street near the Hill School. It is almost inconceivable to us today that this primitive system kept homes and businesses safe from incineration in the early twentieth century.

The Philadelphia Steam Fire Engine Company, established in 1871, acquired this building in 1880 at the corner of Chestnut and Penn Streets. It was constructed with a large bell tower, which allowed the men to see the entire town from their station. This card is from 1910. The "Phillies" have remained at this location.

Today the "Phillies" station looks much like this card from the 1990s.

Also established in 1871, the Goodwill Fire Company made its home on South Hanover Street.

From the same era as the previous view, this card shows the Goodwill Ambulance whose home was next to the fire company. Both of these buildings, now adapted for other uses, are still present on Hanover Street.

The Sanatoga Fire Company's members are gathered here in front of the Sanatoga Post Office building.

Stowe's Fire House, home to the West End Fire Company, is pictured in this early card.

The Sanatoga Pumper is featured in this early card beneath a sign featuring one of Pottstown's old products, Ferro-Phos. The small print says, "Wonderful blood and nerve tonic for sale everywhere."

Upper Pottsgrove has its own fire department as well, located on North Farmington Avenue.

Chapter Eight

Military

Pottstown men and women have never shirked their duty to their country. Prior to World War II, only men served in the military and the women kept the home fires burning. With the outbreak of World War II, women carved out a more proactive role for themselves by enlisting in the armed forces. For those not so daring, working in the defense plants was essential to the winning of the war. Unfortunately, cards depicting the "Rosie the Riveter" of Pottstown do not exist, but her influence was surely felt in this industrial town.

Built in 1910, the National Guard Armory played and continues to play a vital role in the preparedness of military enlistees. Located on King Street, the building exterior remains much the same as on this card. It was originally the home of Company A. Its name has changed but it remains an important military link for the community.

In 1938 the Pottstown Post of the Veterans of Foreign Wars provided a military salute at the funeral of John Boyer, the last Civil War Veteran to be laid to rest in Pottstown.

In 1906, Company A of the Pennsylvania National Guard held a summer military encampment called Camp Warren at Sanatoga. These young men appear young enough to be Boy Scouts.

In their uniforms, the soldiers appear much more mature. This is again from Camp Warren in 1906.

Company A returned victorious after quelling the Mexican Border uprising in 1917. The accolades of the community rained down upon them.

On November 3, 1917, the conscripts for World War I are receiving a farewell at the train station. Please note the photographers on the poles to the left of the scene.

The well-wishers are certainly giving the men a fine sendoff to battle in World War I. This must be at the Pennsylvania Railroad Station as the building to the center rear is the Pottstown Cold Storage Company. Before the home freezer came into wide usage, space could be rented at the Cold Storage Company to store a family's meat or vegetables laid up for the winter. This method of storing took the place of drying or canning those provisions.

Chapter Nine

Public Buildings

What a delightful old mansion the former Pottstown Library was! Working on a term paper, seated in the enclosed porch, was almost a pleasure instead of a chore. Purchased by the Century Club from the Casselberry family in 1920, it remained in use until the 1970s when the former post office building became the new library, affording more space. This site was on High Street next to the Citizen's Bank; and unfortunately, all that remains is a parking lot.

We will be a little late to take advantage of this 1893 invitation to the Opera House.

Located on the north side of King Street between Charlotte and Penn Streets, the Opera House was the civic entertainment center of town for a number of years. Located between the armory and the former city hall, a parking lot has replaced it.

A view from 1922 shows the Opera House before the building of the new city hall.

Apparently the Opera House was still standing in 1930, which is the date on this postal card showing the new city hall on King Street.

The Pottstown YMCA was built in 1913 and provided many services to the men of the area. For some, who came to the area because of employment, it provided a home away from home during the week while they worked in local industry. For others it provided clean recreation and sports in a non-threatening environment. Located on the southwest corner of King and Evans Streets, its bowling alleys caused the streets to rumble many evenings. An annex housing Pottstown's only indoor pool was built in 1922 on the west side of the building providing the opportunity for many to learn swimming.

December 9, 1916 marked the laying of the cornerstone of the new post office (now the library) on the southeast corner of High Street at Washington Street.

This card, mailed in the 1980s, shows the post office as the new library.

This architectural view of the same post office on a linen type card was mailed in 1946.

A very important place affecting the health, safety, and well being of Pottstown's residents is the water treatment plant, pictured here in 1938.

The interior of the Bahr Arcade is shown circa 1910. A poultry show is in session.

Not all hospitals were on a grand scale in the early twentieth century. This graceful home, called Southside, provided the constant care of a physician.

In this photo from the 1960s by noted Pottstown photographer Eugene Orlando, the hospital has been enlarged but the original turrets are still visible. Now an office complex, the building looks much the same as on this card.

The Homeopathic Hospital of Pottstown, on East High Street, opened with a total of sixteen beds in 1916. In 1922, with the help of a capital campaign, the beds increased to twenty-two. Its nursing school was begun shortly after the establishment of the hospital itself.

The Pottstown Hospital's original building was built in 1892 on North Charlotte Street. Its school of nursing began in 1894. In the hospital's first year of operation, ninety-eight patients obtained treatment.

A linen card from the 1940s lends a view of the hospital as many will remember it. This scene is the remodeled building shown on the previous page.

Opening its doors in the 1960s, the Pottstown Memorial Medical Center was formed when the two older hospitals united and combined their resources. The merger incorporated not only the names of the two entities but merged staff as well. This was quite a transition for those who were dedicated to their respective hospitals. Time, it seems, has healed many heartaches present at the time of the merger. The not-for-profit community hospital was acquired several years ago by a corporately structured hospital firm whose ability to purchase in volume, because of its many holdings, helps to keep down the cost of health care.

This is the hospital in the 1960s. Time has moved on and the building currently houses a nursing home.

Chapter Ten

Amusements and Parks

Horse races, poultry shows, dancing, football, baseball, local bands, outstanding high school bands, car races, theater, ice-skating on both the Schuylkill River and the Manatawny Creek, and many more interests captured the fancy of people residing in and near Pottstown in the twentieth century. These next few cards will attempt to show that variation of interests.

The crowd is lined up for the Adams' Ranch Wild West Show at the fair in this card circa 1910.

Come Friday to the Grand Horse Fair at Pottstown Park (Mill Park behind Pottsgrove Manor, occupied now by a shopping center) for only twenty-five cents admission.

It would seem that it was fashionable to appear at the fair in your best clothing, judging from this card of the fair midway circa 1915.

Sulky races were the rage at Mill Park for many years.

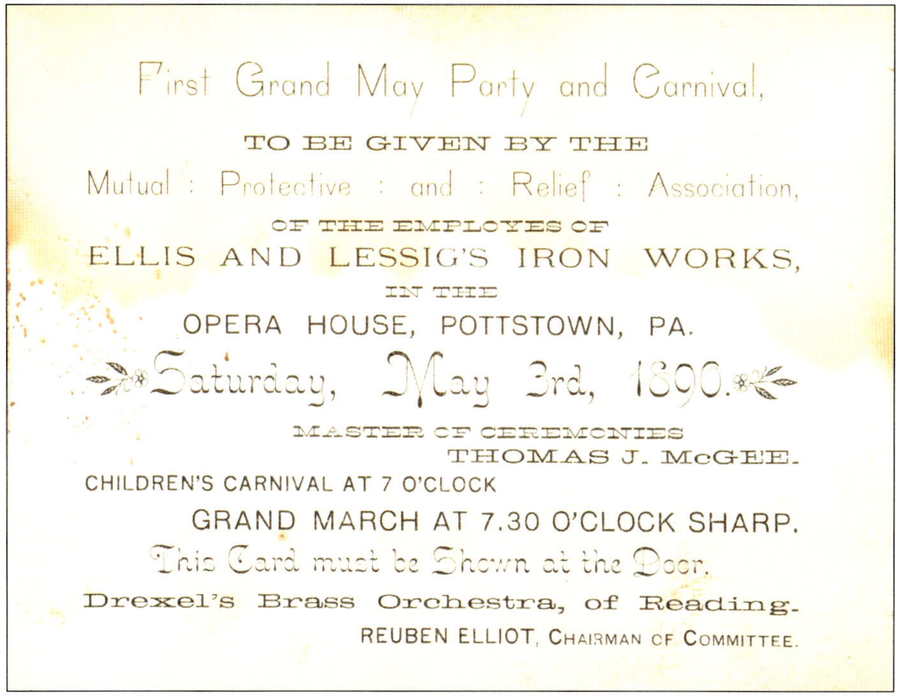
First Grand May Party and Carnival,

TO BE GIVEN BY THE

Mutual : Protective : and : Relief : Association,

OF THE EMPLOYES OF

ELLIS AND LESSIG'S IRON WORKS,

IN THE

OPERA HOUSE, POTTSTOWN, PA.

Saturday, May 3rd, 1890.

MASTER OF CEREMONIES

THOMAS J. McGEE.

CHILDREN'S CARNIVAL AT 7 O'CLOCK

GRAND MARCH AT 7.30 O'CLOCK SHARP.

This Card must be Shown at the Door.

Drexel's Brass Orchestra, of Reading.

REUBEN ELLIOT, CHAIRMAN OF COMMITTEE.

A May Carnival and Party at the Opera House, sponsored by the employees of the Ellis & Lessig's Iron Works to benefit their insurance protection, is proclaimed on this card from 1890.

This 1914 card advertises some sturdy mules to get the farm work done.

An advertising card from 1911 tells of "The Newlyweds & Their Baby" coming to the Opera House on King Street.

The thirty-five piece Pottstown Band is pictured in the Opera House circa 1910.

Ice-skating is being enjoyed at Manatawny Park as seen in this circa 1917 card.

The Junior Girls and Boys Band of about forty members poses proudly for this picture on the steps of the Odd Fellows Hall on King Street circa 1920.

Frank Schatz, Leader, 414 Walnut Street, Pottstown, Pa.

Zeke Meyer appears here in his proclaimed fastest dirt track car at the Pottstown Speedway.

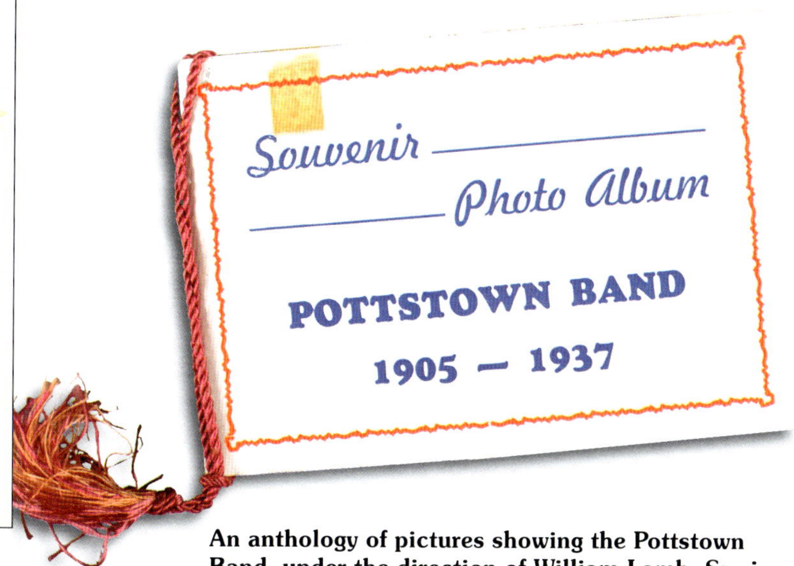

An anthology of pictures showing the Pottstown Band, under the direction of William Lamb, Sr., is chronicled here. His son William Lamb, Jr. assumed the helm in 1937 and continued to bless the town with band music for many years.

These tough young football players pose outside Pottstown High School in 1920.

Summer camps surrounded Pottstown for many years until the advent of housing developments that have managed to gobble up these rustic areas. This card depicts pleasant Camp Fernbrook of North Coventry in the 1950s.

Bobby Shantz, a Pottstown High School graduate hailing from Sanatoga, made it big in the Major Leagues playing for both the Philadelphia Athletics and the New York Yankees. In September 2007, the athletic field at Pottstown High School was named in his honor.

Always good for a refreshing cool-off, the pool at Sunnybrook provided a great playground for swimmers of all ages. Sunnybrook's famed ballroom hosted all the name bands and singers of the Big Band Era. Its surrounding grounds provided large areas for company, church and family picnics. A great place for expos and shows as well as dining, Sunnybrook is now undergoing restoration to bring its beauty and function into the twenty-first century.

Ringing Rocks Park

Just to the north of Pottstown lie the ringing rocks, boulders that when struck with a hammer are capable of producing musical tones. There is disagreement about the origin of these rocks. Were they at the end of a glacier before it receded, or were they formed from volcanic rock upheaval? No one has a definitive answer. What is known is that they and the neighboring wooded area became a great respite for fun, relaxation, picnics, and amusements in the later part of the nineteenth century. Like its counterpart in Sanatoga, this park, too, enjoyed the services of the newly formed trolley lines, which allowed folks ready access to it. This writer has seen evidence that the park promoters had other interests in the park area. Advertisements circulated to entice buyers to purchase lots creating a housing development of sorts. Some summer cottages, now year round residences, were constructed. Over the years many homes have been built in the area.

Add on glitter was used to enhance and sell this Independence Day greeting from the park.

This trestle view shows the large roller coaster that people loved to ride.

And come they did, from Pottstown, Boyertown, and the other towns along the trolley route. This shows one of the trestles over which the trolley traversed.

A very early real photo card enables us to see the W. S. Lord Restaurant at the park, where a light lunch of oysters and clams is featured in fine print on the marquee. It is uncertain if that is Mr. Lord on top of the restaurant. Again, the roller coaster is visible.

This gentleman is seen guarding the entrance to the cave.

This collection of rocks looks today very much as this old postcard depicts them.

In the years of its popularity as an amusement park, names were given to the various rock formations. 1906 is the date on this German Rotograph of the Haystack.

Although looking rather uncomfortable, it is easy to see how Sofa Rock got its name.

Ringing Rocks Park was known as a great place to hold picnics. The men and women of the Keystone Fire Company of Boyertown seem to be enjoying an afternoon of fun, captured in this early photo card.

This card was postmarked in 1909. Someone had a very vivid imagination to label this formation Umbrella and Oven Rock.

This is a real photo card showing the original park building before the restoration to what we know today as Ringing Rocks Roller Skating Rink.

Over one hundred years later young people still come to Ringing Rocks to socialize, and now to roller skate at one of the few remaining rinks in the area. This card portrays a nice view of the skating floor.

Souvenirs are always popular and this is one of a very few tangible pieces remaining today. This planter dates from about the 1920s.

Mr. Lachman of Pottstown gladly took pictures of visitors to the park. He had a well-patronized photography studio in town.

Sanatoga Park

Sanatoga Park, constructed in the late nineteenth century, consisted of forty acres of woodland and a lake. Its location just east of the village of Sanatoga made it about a two-mile excursion from Pottstown. It lay at the base of Crooked Hill, which is the meaning of Sanatoga in the Lenni Lenape language. With the advent of the trolley lines serving Pottstown and other communities, it soon became a gathering place of note for many family outings, a great dating mecca, a place to meet new friends, and a wonderful place for organizational picnics. The postcards in this section tell the park's story.

This photo is taken from an old souvenir book of the park.

Meet at the corner of High and Evans Streets in Pottstown and the trolley will take you to a bingo party in the auditorium at Sanatoga Park says this card from 1900. This does not seem too radically different from taking a bus ride to a casino in Atlantic City today!

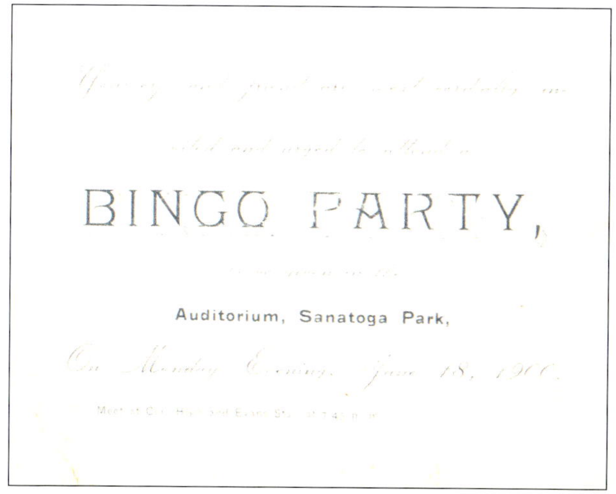

The fine auditorium or pavilion shown here featured a large and spacious dance floor that could accommodate up to 2,000 people under roof and kept them protected from storms while offering plenty of ventilation for coolness. Dancing ran every day but Sunday and music was free for afternoon outings. Dancing carnivals, masquerades, and novelty dances were featured during the season. The veranda held seating for five hundred or more.

The Longview Resort offered rooms should folks wish to stay and visit the park for a period of days. This card is pre 1907.

A rustic bridge over the lake is pictured in this German photograph taken sometime prior to 1920.

The bridge and spillway of the dam breast are seen here. Engineered by George F. P. Wanger, the lake obviously filled. There were some skeptics who doubted his design, and to whom he replied, "If it doesn't fill, you don't owe me anything."

Once inside the park, Lake Sanatoga was a featured stop. One half mile long and three hundred feet wide, it was a delight to navigate with a rented boat or canoe from one of the boathouses pictured. The Napha Launch took up to eighteen people for rides on the lake. A swimming pool, having a sand and gravel bottom, with diving and sliding boards made "it a comfort and pleasure to bathe in this cool exhilarating body of water, which was absolutely clean." So the Sanatoga Lake brochure stated!

Several handsome young men seem to be taking a breather from the park activities or perhaps are awaiting some young lady friends to join them.

By far the biggest attraction for those thrill seekers had to be the roller coaster.

More than just a water park and a dance hall, Sanatoga Park drew the interest of the real thrill seekers with its attractions and rides. This view from the 1920s shows both the lake and some rides.

This much later photograph shows a variety of park amusements. A carousel, whip, shooting gallery, Kentucky Derby, high slide, aeroplane, huckly buck, high striker, and rolling ball were just a few of the many entertainments afforded the park goers.

Chapter Eleven

Celebrations

Like people in most places of the United States, the folks of Pottstown have never passed up an opportunity to celebrate holidays in many ways. After all, everyone loves a parade!

This picture card was done at Christmastime at High and Hanover Streets looking north prior to 1926. We know that because Trinity Church still has its tall steeple, which was destroyed by a storm in 1926.

A patriotic parade is shown moving east on High Street near Charlotte. The Bahr Building, or more commonly the Bahr Arcade, is pictured on the left, and in the distance on the left is the Security Building.

This card proclaims the pride in their endeavors that these firemen of the Philadelphia Steam Fire Engine Company #1 celebrate by walking and riding on their new motorized fire engine.

At still another parade at about the same spot, the Modern Woodmen are having their day.

The "Trip Around the World" appears to be starting in front of the Trinity Church. Those internal or "infernal" combustion engines seem to be producing a large amount of smoke.

The Eagles Arch is shown here, across from their fraternal home on High Street, looking west toward the Bahr Arcade.

Apparently Flag Day is being celebrated in this 1908 card picturing the Philadelphia Fire Company Band.

Chapter Twelve

Fraternal Orders and Lodges

It has been said of the nineteenth and early twentieth centuries that a man in good standing in his community could be out every night of the week to attend one meeting or another. The Odd Fellows, Owls, Elks, Patriotic Sons of America, Masons, Templars, Knights of the Golden Eagle, Modern Woodmen, the Grange, various political groups, and the American Legion were just some of the many organizations that proliferated during this era. Of course, some are still active today.

The Independent Order of Odd Fellows' Hall, shown in 1914 with patriotic trappings, stood on the south side of King Street near Charlotte Street where an apartment complex has now replaced it.

The ladies were invited to attend the First Grand Dress Ball at the Odd Fellows' Hall in 1856. The costuming would be elegant and priceless if seen in today's antique market.

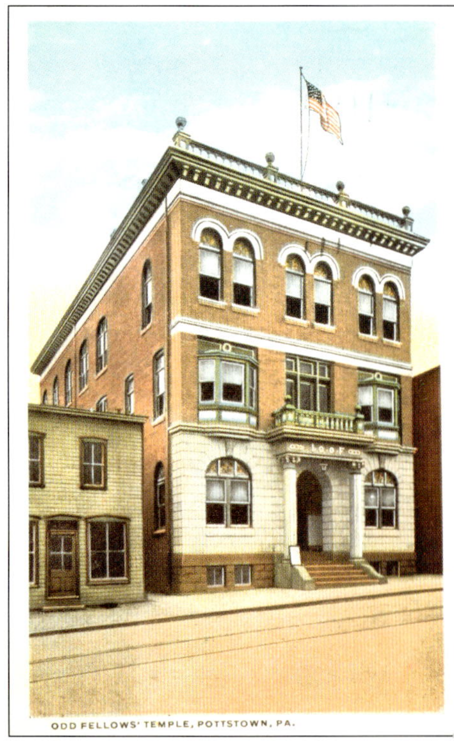

Those old enough to remember this building will perhaps remember its appearance as in this view from 1933. Miss Evelyn Shelly's elocution classes were held here for many years. The small building to the left held a tin and hardware shop.

In 1861 The Washington Troop held a Dress Ball at the Madison House at the corner of High and Keim Streets.

In 1894 the Anniversary Entertainment for the Knights of the Golden Eagle included mandolin and cornet selections, vocal duets, as well as a few recitations.

Another invitation to a Grand Ball was issued in 1892 by the Pottstown Republican Pioneer Corps. It is believed that Porter's Hall was also on High Street.

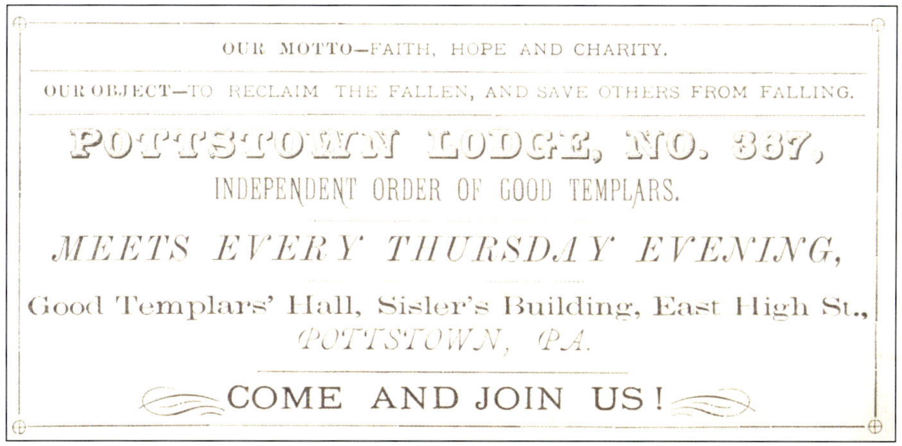

All were invited to the Good Templars meeting "to reclaim the fallen, and save others from falling."

On the North Coventry side of the river the Norco Grange, or Farmer's Hall, in Cedarville is seen here also prior to 1915. The grange organization began in 1867 after the Civil War in the United States and spread across rural America. A group formed in North Coventry in the late nineteenth century. The grange was designed to be of service to farming families. Urban development has taken its toll on granges throughout the United States and certainly in this area. This hall is now home to Cedarville Boy Scout Troop #95 whose members use the ground floor for their meetings. Owned by the Cedarville United Methodist Church, the second floor is used for their youth outreach programs. This card was a sample to a local country store.

This Pottstown Aerie #626 of the Fraternal Order of Eagles program dates from 1908 and featured a concert, a May pole dance, and a dance program consisting of thirty numbers with thirty minute intermissions after each six selections.

On a postcard prior to 1915 the Modern Woodmen are pictured marching up High Street. This postcard offers a splendid view of the business establishments on the north side of High Street between Penn and Hanover Streets.

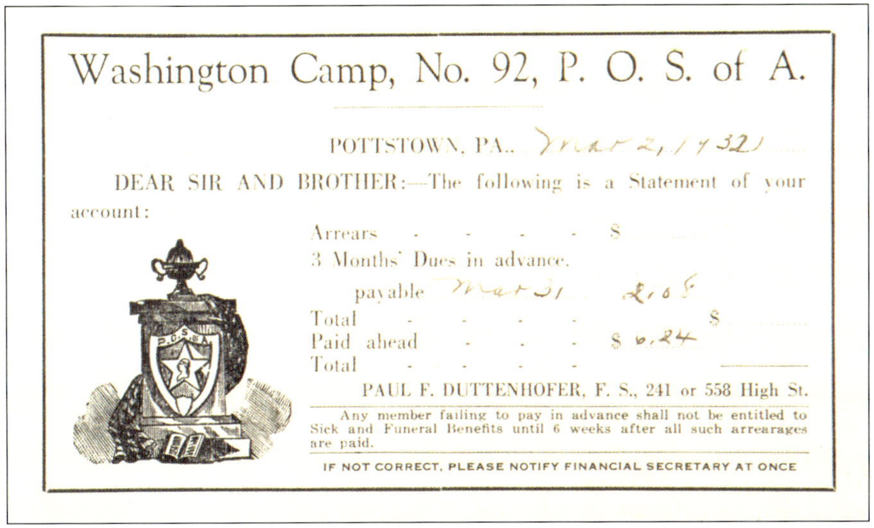

Washington Camp, No. 92, P. O. S. of A.

POTTSTOWN, PA., Mar 2, 1932

DEAR SIR AND BROTHER:—The following is a Statement of your account:

Arrears - - - - $

3 Months' Dues in advance.

payable Mar 31 2.08

Total - - - - $

Paid ahead - - - $ 6.24

Total - - - -

PAUL F. DUTTENHOFER, F. S., 241 or 558 High St.

Any member failing to pay in advance shall not be entitled to Sick and Funeral Benefits until 6 weeks after all such arrearages are paid.

IF NOT CORRECT, PLEASE NOTIFY FINANCIAL SECRETARY AT ONCE

A 1932 dues card from the Patriotic Order Sons of America is shown here.

A fine old mansion near the corner of Franklin and King Streets was the home of the George A. Amole American Legion Post #47 until their new building was constructed next to this one. A small corner of the Schumacher & Reber Funeral Home can be seen in the bottom left.

The old Fegely mansion on High Street just west of York Street became the home of the Elks Club in Pottstown and is shown here circa 1920. The Elks and other civic groups in town still use its gracious rooms for meetings. Many receptions and parties have been held within its walls over the years.

Chapter Thirteen

Religion

Just as Pottstown was a diverse town in the development of industry using labor from many portions of the world, it stands to reason that it was diversified in its religious beliefs of those people. The founder, John Potts, and many of his English business associates in those early days were Quakers who felt the influence of the best-known English Friend of all, namely William Penn, and later his sons. The Society of Friends in colonial Pottstown had a relationship with the Exeter meeting and visiting Quakers would conduct services when in the vicinity. A Quaker meetinghouse constructed in 1875 is no longer standing. Its location was on King Street east of Hanover Street.

A very heavy influence on the religious community of early Pottstown was the German based Protestant sects. The Lutheran and Reformed Churches had a profound impact on early Pottsgrove. The "Old Brick Church," now Zion's United Church of Christ at the corner of Hanover and Chestnut Streets, is the matriarch of many Pottstown churches. The congregation of this church began meeting in 1769 and erected the church in 1796. It has been the meeting place and origin for a number of local congregations, some leaving to establish services in German or English or as separate Lutheran or Reformed parishes. The local Catholics, who for a time had no building in which to worship, came to the "Old Brick Church" as well, until their church home was completed. As the town grew so did ethnic diversity even among the Catholic population. They wished to worship among people with whom they shared a common heritage.

The Jewish community of Pottstown had its origin in the mid 1800s when a large influx of German and Middle European peoples immigrated to the United States. Among these new arrivals to America were a few Jewish merchants who built businesses in Pottstown. Near the end of the nineteenth century, Russian and Polish Jews came to the area. Previously meeting in homes of its members, the Jewish community's first public religious home was on Hale Street in 1889 for the "Brotherly Love" congregation. In 1892, the "Mercy of Truth" congregation took over the synagogue. The year of 1926 saw the dedication of the new synagogue on High Street, and in 1962, their present building on North Keim Street was completed and dedicated.

This is a real photo card from before 1907 showing the "Old Brick Church" — Pottstown's "Mother Church."

Among the last to leave the Zion Church was the Emmanuel Lutheran congregation in 1872. This church has the largest Protestant congregation in town and is pictured here in 1909.

Emmanuel Lutheran is shown here much as it appears today from Hanover Street. A horrible storm in 1878 brought down the steeple and the congregation opted not to rebuild it.

Speaking of tall steeples, shown here is the steeple of the Trinity Reformed Church completed in 1869. Trinity, another offshoot of the Zion Church, it is now a part of the United Church of Christ denomination.

This photo bears testimony to the devastation suffered by the Trinity Church after being struck by lightning in 1926.

An architect's drawing captures the beauty of the new St. James Lutheran Church at High and Price Streets. This congregation is another of Zion's spawns.

The Lutheran Church of the Transfiguration also had its inception at the Zion Church. It was formed in1848 originally as an English Lutheran congregation and it became a combined English-German congregation in 1867. The members completed this edifice in 1869 and this view is from 1908. It is now home to the Invictus Congregation.

A view of the First Presbyterian Church from the 1930s is presented here. A congregation, who had its origins in 1848, built the church in 1889. Strong ties to the Hill School and the Meigs family aided the early parishioners' efforts in the growth of their church. No longer at High and Evans Streets, the church moved to the North End in the 1960s.

This is the interior of the old St. James Lutheran Church on Green Street above High Street.

Methodist circuit riders came to Pottstown as early as 1740, and continued into the middle of the nineteenth century. The congregation of the First Methodist Church, organized in 1867, built their sturdy building on High Street in 1871. The lovely parsonage was razed for the construction of a church school building.

This advertisement proclaims the visit of a girl evangelist to the First Methodist Church.

Christ Episcopal Church was built in 1872. It has undergone several renovations since then. This card is from 1908. The congregation had its beginning about 1825 and it, too, met in the "Old Brick Church." It is one of the few local churches that hosts the Cluster Outreach Luncheons served by volunteers from many of the community's churches.

The congregation of the Searles Memorial Methodist Church had its beginnings in Glasgow, just north of Pottstown. They moved to Pottstown in 1889 where they named themselves the 5th Street Methodist Church, having moved to Fifth and York Streets. Requiring more room, they moved to Hanover and Beech Streets in 1911. The Heart of God Church now occupies this building.

Grace Evangelical Lutheran Church is another of Zion's children. This 1908 card shows its building on West Street. It has since moved to North Charlotte Street where its buildings command nearly one-half of a city block.

Shown is St. Peter's Lutheran Church in Stowe. It was a mission church of Emmanuel Lutheran.

St. Paul's Reformed Church in Stowe had its beginnings from a Sunday school begun by the Trinity Reformed Congregation.

The congregation of the First Baptist Church met in the Armory just up the street from their present church at King and Charlotte Streets for one year. In 1911, they marched down King Street praising God for their new home, where they remain today.

The First Baptist Church has a unique history. It was born as a result of a funeral! Catharine Pennypacker, of North Coventry Township, had passed away. The pastor from the Lower Providence Baptist Church was called to officiate and drew such a crowd that more Baptist meetings were held subsequently in the town hall. In February of 1857, after they cut through the ice, twenty-two people came for baptism in the Schuylkill River. Thousands of onlookers shivered on the banks. This is the old meetinghouse used until 1910.

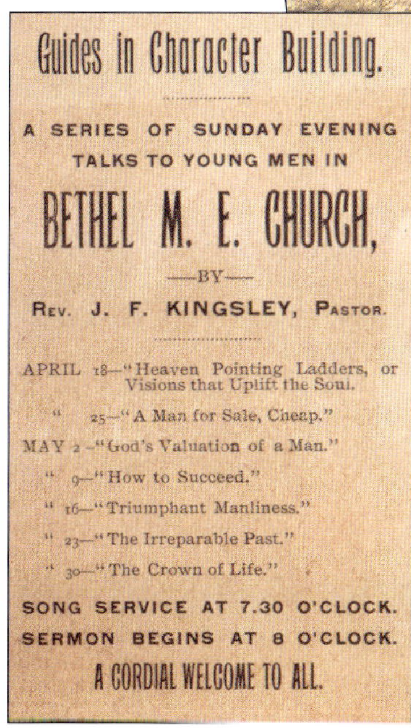

Guides in Character Building.

A SERIES OF SUNDAY EVENING TALKS TO YOUNG MEN IN

BETHEL M. E. CHURCH,

—BY—

REV. J. F. KINGSLEY, PASTOR.

APRIL 18—"Heaven Pointing Ladders, or Visions that Uplift the Soul."
" 25—"A Man for Sale, Cheap."
MAY 2—"God's Valuation of a Man."
" 9—"How to Succeed."
" 16—"Triumphant Manliness."
" 23—"The Irreparable Past."
" 30—"The Crown of Life."

SONG SERVICE AT 7.30 O'CLOCK.
SERMON BEGINS AT 8 O'CLOCK.

A CORDIAL WELCOME TO ALL.

Bethel Methodist Episcopal Church offered talks on character building as noted on this card in the early twentieth century. Their church was organized in 1871 at the corner of Franklin and Beech Streets.

1912 is the date on the postmark of this card depicting St. Aloysious Roman Catholic Church. In early times Catholics had to travel at least thirteen miles to attend a Catholic service or be content with attending Protestant services with their neighbors, many at the "Old Brick Church." In 1856, with the influx of many more Catholic workers who were connected with the construction of railroads, a church was built on the present site of St. Aloysius. The edifice, as we know it, was built in 1891 and the parochial school in 1913.

The Trinity Evangelical Congregational Church and its pastor grace this 1904 calendar picture. Trinity Church was a presence at the corner of Franklin and Walnut Streets from 1893. The Church of the Living God now holds services there.

St. John the Baptist Greek Catholic Church is on Cherry Street between Charlotte and Evans Streets. Its Slavic type dome is easy to spot from the Industrial Highway.

The congregation of Holy Trinity Slavic Roman Catholic Church had this fine edifice constructed in 1912 on South Street. This card was mailed in 1910, but is of pre-1907 vintage.

This is the way the Congregation Mercy and Truth Synagogue looked on High Street at Warren Street from 1925 until the 1960s. The building was razed and the site is now home to a financial institution.

On South Keim Street in North Coventry, the Coventry Brethren Church holds the distinction of being the oldest continuous Church of the Brethren in America. Begun by Martin Urner in 1714, its building has undergone transition from a log cabin to a lovely church with numerous renovations. This card dates probably from the 1950s.

The Cedarville United Methodist Church had its beginnings in 1873 when ground was given the congregation by George Wanger, a neighboring farmer — not of the Methodist faith. This pre 1907 card shows the early church before renovations and additions.

Shenkel United Church of Christ had its beginnings in 1837 when it was known as the Second German Reformed Church of North Coventry. This, too, is a pre 1907 view of the church. In the mid 1800s this church was the unlikely scene of a demonstration of nudity one Sunday morning during worship. A religious sect called the "Battleaxes" gave notice to their neighbors that they were sincere in their own beliefs of sharing one's marital partner. The "Battleaxes" presence in the neighboring villages of Shenkel and Cedarville was not long-lived. But, that very presence caused church pastors and others great concern for the welfare of villagers' family life. Some family units were literally torn apart by this strange cult. After the brutal axe murder of one of the cult members and the subsequent trial of some others, the leading members of the sect moved on leaving several very disturbed and torn apart communities. These feelings persisted through several generations until it seems "time heals all wounds."

Chapter Fourteen

Schools

Schools in Pottstown have existed since the later part of the eighteenth century when in 1785 a private school was built at Walnut and Penn Streets near the "Old Brick Church." Of log construction, it was in use until 1841 when it was demolished. In 1834 a private academy for tuition paying students was built on Chestnut Street between Hanover and Penn Streets. Ironically 1834 was the same year that the Public School Law of Pennsylvania was enacted. This law was not well accepted in its time because it allowed taxation of the populace to fund the schools. Somehow this sounds all too familiar today. A two-count majority allowed the vote to build public schools in Pottstown to pass and two small brick schools were constructed.

In 1854 the Streeper Building was erected on Penn Street between Chestnut and Walnut Streets. This two story, four-roomed building served as a high school. In the fifty-year span between 1838 and 1888 a number of new elementary schools were constructed within the borough. In 1889 with an extension of the borough limits, more schools were added within the actual town itself along with the Stowe and Glasgow areas. With more students taking advantage of higher education, a new high school was built on Beech Street at Penn Street. For the first time in Pottstown, boys and girls were united in this new secondary school. Fire consumed this building in 1933.

This fine picture, taken prior to 1907, is of the no longer existing Washington School Building built in 1887 as part of the Pottstown School District.

Also part of the Pottstown Schools, in 1908 this was known as the Richards Building.

South Keim and South Streets are home to this early Pottstown elementary school. The Grant School is now utilized as the home of the Pottstown Eagles fraternal organization.

The Rupert Elementary School is shown shortly after its completion in 1927. Discussions are currently under way regarding major renovations to the school or its demolition and the construction of a new school to replace it.

The Pottstown Junior High School was built in 1923 and currently serves the middle school population of the community.

This sweet little plate, made in Germany and depicting the local high school, was an advertising giveaway by a local business.

This is a 1920s vintage postcard of the Pottstown High School that was built in 1892 serving both male and female students for the first time in one building.

The Pottstown Senior High School, which many of the older readers of this book may remember, was constructed in 1923 facing Chestnut Street between Hanover and Penn Streets. It was used as a middle school before its demise and the creation of a parking lot in its place.

Evidence of the disastrous fire that destroyed the old high school in 1933 is depicted in this old photograph.

North Coventry had a number of early country schools. This one, now housing a church in Pottstown Landing, was built about 1859 on the farm of George Wanger and is where his wife Rebecca Price Wanger was the first teacher. The ground and building, given to the township about 1868, lie just west of the current Coventry Mall. The original building is to the rear of the church constructed on Laurelwood Road.

This great aerial view from 1968 shows the newly constructed Pottstown High School in the upper center, the Pottstown Middle School to the right, Grace Lutheran Church, the current Manorcare Nursing Home and the First Presbyterian Church.

A 1914 class of youngsters is pictured with their teacher at the Pottstown Landing School.

This fine schoolhouse, built in later part of the nineteenth century, stands in Cedarville, North Coventry Township. This view shows youngsters of the 1920s judging from their dress. The school is now a beautiful residence.

An early postcard depicts the old West Pottsgrove High School in Stowe. West, Upper and Lower Pottsgrove united to form the Pottsgrove School System, in the mid 1950s, with their new high school located in Upper Pottsgrove just beyond the city limits of Pottstown.

The North Coventry High School was constructed in the early 1900s and is pictured here circa 1914. North Coventry Township merged with the townships of South and East Coventry, East and West Vincent, and Warwick to form the Owen J. Roberts School District, graduating their first class in 1956. This building remained as a 4th and 5th grade center for the district until a few years ago when a new North Coventry Elementary School was built. It, along with the old elementary school behind it, is now home to the West-Mont Christian Academy.

This very old, pre 1907, postcard gives evidence of the Ringing Hill School House. It is not clear if this became the site of the present Ringing Rocks Elementary School or had another place within Upper Pottsgrove.

The Lower Pottsgrove Township Elementary School on Pleasantview Road just north of Sanatoga is shown here. Upon construction of a new public elementary school, this building became home to the Coventry Christian School.

St. Aloysius Parochial School on Hanover Street is pictured on this card probably from the 1920s judging from its white border. The school is a part of the St. Aloysius Roman Catholic Church seen to the right and was built in 1913.

The pupils of the Sanatoga School are pictured in 1912.

This photo card from the 1960s, taken by Eugene Orlando, shows the St. Pius X High School on Keim Street in Lower Pottsgrove.

Pottstown is very fortunate to be graced by one of the finest preparatory schools in the country, namely The Hill School. Originally established as a school for young men, it has been a coed facility for several years and educates young people from the Third through the Sixth Form (ninth through twelfth grades). Matthew Meigs, the Presbyterian pastor and former president of the University of Delaware, created it in 1851. Meigs started the school in a home begun by David Potts in 1793. It was John Meigs, Matthew's son, who is credited with making the school a successful operation. The Hill draws its students from a worldwide clientele, as well as locally, and prepares them for matriculation to the finest colleges and universities. Fields of endeavor such as law, medicine, government, business, and the arts have had splendid Hill School Alumni additions to them. The private Wyncroft School of Pottstown had its beginnings on the grounds of The Hill School. Since 1925 Wyncroft has had its own school on Rosedale Drive.

A German printed postcard from the 1907-1913 era finds The Hill School greatly enlarged from its humble beginnings.

This pre 1907 card shows a very early residence on the Hill School grounds. It is felt that this was the old Potts' home where the school began.

An architectural drawing of the chapel on the Hill School grounds is printed on a private mailing card placing its date of origin between 1898 and 1901.

This card from the 1960s era, taken by Gene Orlando, shows the chapel as it looked in later years.

The ivy covered Upper School is shown here in the 1920s. The school used to admit boys from grades eight through twelve or second through sixth form. As with any high school seniors, the sixth formers were notorious for their antics including playing rock music through the bell tower speakers, impromptu car shows of their masters' (teachers') autos being hand carried into a building, and unsanctioned trips off campus to such diverse places as Florida by train. Needless to say, if caught graduation was not an option!

More of The Hill's buildings are captured in this early card. Many local residents have never even seen the grounds of the school. The exception is they who ice skate on the school rink during the Winter Holiday vacation period when the school is closed for students.

A card from the 1920s shows Memorial Hall.

Chapter Fifteen

Homes

How often has it been said, "A man's home is his castle?" Homes in Pottstown range from early farmhouses, which can be found within the limits of the old Pottsgrove of John Potts, to the upscale mansion homes of the early industrial pioneers. From duplexes, or half doubles, to apartments, all qualify as a castle to someone. In some instances, it may be a stepping up, non-permanent dwelling, but never-the-less, it is his or her castle while that person resides there.

Many of these homes are still standing on High Street looking west from Warren.

Annie Richards was an early Pottsgrove resident whose home was on High Street near Hanover. The home appears to be a very early farmhouse with additions. It was razed to make way for businesses.

Another view of East High Street from the 1930s is pictured here.

Victorian gingerbread adorns this house also noted to be on High Street.

Apparently gracious living abounded on High Street as another view portrays.

Architects from Philadelphia designed this lovely residence.

This card, believed to be from the 1920s, pictures a Kentucky bungalow.

A tenant house along the canal in North Coventry Township is represented on this card.

This view is looking south on Laurelwood Road, North Coventry, at the intersection of West Cedarville Road. The road to the left leads to Cedarville United Methodist Church. Laurelwood Road, itself, follows an old Lenape trail leading from the river, over Chestnut Hill to what is now Ridge Road.

There were deep snows during this winter in Cedarville. The view is looking east on West Cedarville Road.

This card from circa 1917 is showing a nice view of the homes on West Cedarville Road looking east toward Sheep Hill Road.

A few homes and the schoolhouse on West Main Street, South Pottstown, are shown here. Since its days as a schoolhouse, it has been home to several businesses.

One of the earliest homes in North Coventry is pictured here. Ulrich Longenecker came from that part of Europe from which so many early settlers emigrated, namely the German and Swiss countryside. The procurement of land came easily from William Penn's sons who had much of it to sell. The card states that he purchased the land from them in 1736, so this home dates to at least 1740 or earlier. Judging by the rooflines one is led to the conclusion that the original home was just one-half of the size shown in this picture.

An Upper Pottsgrove home on North Farmington Avenue is featured on this card.

Chapter Sixteen

Inns, Hotels, and Restaurants

Good food, good drink and good lodging were always important to the vitality and growth of any community whether for its resident members to enjoy, to entice new business and growth or to house workers not yet married and settled into property ownership. Pottstown was no exception to this. Early postcards demonstrate this fact.

A card from circa 1910 shows the Commercial Hotel with its bar downstairs and living quarters above. It states that Johnny, Carrie, and their children are pictured.

The Buttonwood Hotel, noted to be on High and Washington Streets, preceded the American House.

The American House stood for many years on High Street at Washington Street. Judging from the horse drawn vehicles parked around it, it was a popular spot in the late 1800s as well. The smaller sign above the decorative overhang advertises a hardware store located on the western side of the building.

The Sanatoga Inn, once a trolley stop for the Sanatoga Park, has remained a restaurant serving fine meals to this day. It opened about 1790 as the Crooked Hill Tavern. In 1814 it was a one-story building nestled along the Sanatoga Creek. Various owners added to the building as business prospered in the 1800s. For the last generation, it has been known as Cutillo's Restaurant.

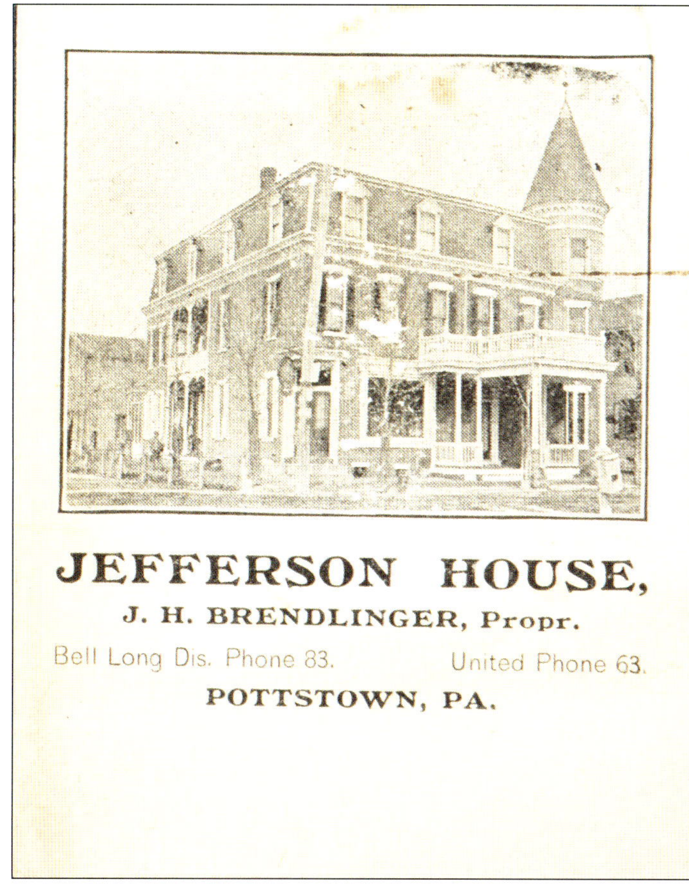

The Jefferson House at the corner of Jefferson Avenue and Charlotte Street remains today as an apartment building.

The East End Hotel, later the Pleasant View Hotel, is shown here about 1910. It was home to the Pottstown Post Office extension in Sanatoga for many years until its recent demise at the hands of the wrecking ball to make way for more modern businesses in Sanatoga. Over the years of its existence it was a center for meetings. It even had a barbershop, a cattle yard, a barroom, a restaurant and an ice cream parlor in times past.

The advertisement speaks for itself. The Merchants Hotel, at the southwest corner of High and York Streets, had everything. Its demise came in the 1960 Johnson redevelopment era when it was demolished to build a restaurant that, despite ownership and name changes, remains today.

A colored card from 1915 shows the Merchants Hotel in all its glory. It stood on the site of the "Rising Sun Hotel," a hostelry, dating from colonial times, where it is said George Washington stopped on his way to stamp out the Whiskey Rebellion in western Pennsylvania. The razing of the Rising Sun occurred in 1865.

Not all of the Merchants Hotel business was geared to humankind. This handsome stud came there every Friday to meet young ladies of his kind for a fee, "insuring a live foal for $15 or $10 for the season." He was a busy young stud being at home at Seven Stars, Chester County, one day a week, one day in Pottstown, and the remainder in Boyertown.

Fine dining was always assured at the Shuler House, built on the site of the former Farmer's Hotel on High Street. Under the ownership of the Govatos family, the Shuler House offered excellent food well into the twentieth century. Now the open lot left by its razing in the 1960s as part of the redevelopment era is part of the City Hall complex.

Howard Johnson's Restaurant located on east High Street at Beech Street drew large crowds for dinner, especially on weekends. The restaurant was a popular place in the 1940s and 1950s for family dining.

Typical of diners of the post World War II era, the Rosedale Diner was a popular establishment. After its usefulness peaked and the ground sold, the diner itself made its home in North Coventry where it received popularity once more as "The Abandoned Luncheonette" pictured on the album of the same name by Daryl Hall and John Oates, the contemporary rock and soul singers. Daryl is a native of North Coventry and credits much of his early musical knowledge and appreciation to groups in and around Pottstown.

Laurel Locks Tea Room flourished in the mid twentieth century in North Coventry south of Route 724 on the east side of South Hanover Street.

The Blossom Restaurant on North Charlotte Street provided good meals to the people of town for many years. Ownership and names have changed but it has continued as a restaurant.

Also located in Upper Pottsgrove Township, the Half-Way House is an old hotel so named because of its distance between Pottstown and Boyertown. Check the vintage cars on this card, which is pre-1962.

Rock's Drive-in located in North Coventry and the Tropical Treat located in Stowe were popular long before fast food restaurants. They are shown here on an ad card, pre-1962 (no zip code), for Slump Brick siding, a fashionable building material of the time.

The Village Diner of Douglassville retains it atmosphere despite remodeling and ownership changes since the 1960s.

Unmistakably quaint prior to 1962 as pictured on this card, the Lakeside Inn still offers good food in a dramatically remodeled building.

The Manatawny Motor Inn located at High and Manatawny Streets offered food and lodging in the 1960s. A motel remains on this site.

The Downtown Motor Inn was another owner of this site.

Sunnybrook Ballroom featured a venue for banquets, conferences, high school proms, entertainment, expos and so much more. Having fallen into disrepair, it is due to reopen sometime soon when renovations are completed. The community has sadly missed it for a number of years.

Chapter Seventeen

Businesses and Street Scenes

High Street has always been the primary place of retail business in Pottstown. Its one hundred foot wide street, planned by John Potts, made it a perfect avenue for the growth of a viable commercial economy in its early years. Its heyday, from the turn of the twentieth century to just past mid-century, is chronicled here along with advertising cards for various businesses seen on the cards or that have been known to exist during this era. Obviously, there are many businesses which thrived but to whom no tribute can be given due to the lack of cards. Some of the businesses were not on High Street or even in Pottstown, but of the area, and they will be included as well.

The old Pottstown Brewing Company on High Street just southeast of the Manatawny Bridge put out his ad card with a lovely child on the reverse. This building has undergone many renovations and owners through the years and now is part of the Montgomery County Community College Campus.

J. Fegely and Son Hardware began their business on High Street just west of the Merchants Hotel. This old photo shows their horse drawn delivery wagon.

Fegely's Hardware Store had many advertising cards which must have paid off as they moved their business to a larger location on the southeast corner of High and York Streets. No longer in that location, they have remained in business to this day, just west of Stowe.

W. Auchenbach's China Palace shared the same address as the jewelry business.

For many years, the Auchenbach Apartments housed the Fritz Grocery on its first floor.

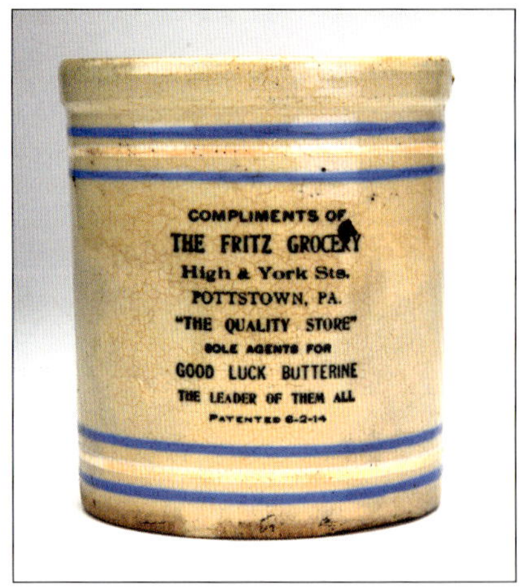

Crecelius, the jeweler, was a busy man selling not only jewelry but watches, clocks and spectacles, complete with eye testing.

Leonard Surg occupied 129 High Street where he sold baked goods.

Weitzenkorn's at 145 High Street is pictured here in 1892. Its location has not changed, making it the longest continually operating store in town.

Imagine a dress shoe for $3.50! The Newark Shoe Store sold them at 141 High Street.

Fashions have changed in over one hundred years, however.

The north 100 block of High Street shows the Weitzenkorn Store mid block. Razed for the construction of a bank, most of the buildings shown on the right of the card are now gone.

Just a few doors east of Weitzenkorn's, the Up to Date Grocery had its establishment. Its lovely old delivery wagon, complete with advertisements for Sleepy Eye Flour and Old Glory Coffee, catches our eyes here.

There is just so much to see in this wonderful old interior postcard of Bentz's Drug Store; from the marble soda counter, its flavoring bottles, the lighting fixtures, the radiator in the middle of the walkway to the caged area presumably where the pharmacist did the compounding of his formulary of medications. Bentz's Drug Store, a favorite lunch stop for many high-school students at the corner of High and Hanover Streets, was among those torn down.

This is the bank that replaced all the businesses on the corner. Gene Orlando did this card from the 1960s.

Looking south on Hanover Street, this card embraces the buildings still remaining at King and Hanover Streets as well as the area now covered by the Patriot Bank.

Built in 1897 by Jacob Fegely, the Security Building has just undergone major renovations for office rentals. The original bank's use of marble counters and brass teller shields harkened to an era long gone.

This photo shows the interior of the store before the move across Hanover Street to their current location.

A favorite stop for many years for many people, Sheridans sold hot roasted peanuts, local newspapers, newspapers from other towns and cities, cigars, cigarettes and other tobacco products. There were even shoeshine chairs in the earlier store.

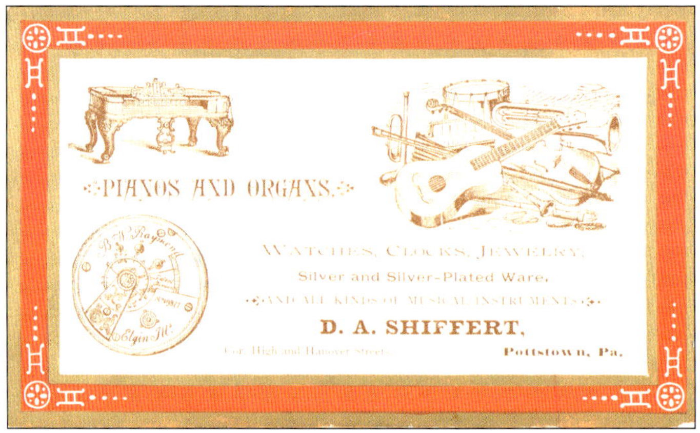

Located at the corner of High and Hanover Streets in the late 1800s, Mr. Shiffert's store sold a wide variety of goods.

This view is of the south side of High Street from Hanover to Charlotte Streets.

General Arthur St.Clair's home at the corner of High and Hanover Streets had been turned into a commercial establishment by the late 1800s. Seen here in 1911, its conversion to a theater and a store is quite evident.

The north side of High Street in the same block is shown.

A later and closer view of the south side of High Street reveals the new Hippodrome Theater, a great childhood favorite for its showing of westerns every Saturday. In addition, VanBuskirk & Bros. Hardware is seen. Long a mainstay on High Street, it held several locations. This card also shows the St.Clair House at the corner of High and Hanover Streets.

How prophetic was the title marquee at the Hippodrome Theater in 1958! "The Day the West Burst into Flame" promotes the film "From Hell to Texas" while the local firefighters are quelling a blaze next door. This picture affords a nice view of the High Street stores at that time including Levitz, Van Buskirk and Sears Roebuck.

For the tidy housekeeper, this "lovely" set of sad irons could be purchased at VanBuskirks. Is it any wonder they called them sad irons? If the opportunity arises to lift one, the reason will be readily apparent.

S. Miller gave out this card in the late 1800s. His store later moved to the northeast corner of High and Hanover Streets. Their business, too, lasted well over one hundred years into the late 1900s.

Just up the street, a mid twentieth century photo shows smoke from a third floor apartment. This was before the construction of the façade covering those windows.

Trout's Music Store at 210 High Street sold all types of musical instruments, sewing machines, and phonographs at the beginning of the twentieth century.

One never tires of studying the interiors of these great old soda fountains. This one is of Burdan's Dining Parlor at 209 High Street, across the street from Trout's Music Store.

George R. Harrison advertised his wares with this card.

Ellis Mills, a fine department store on High Street, carried the latest fashions and house wares. Its building featured an overhead tube system to carry the proceeds from sales directly to the second floor office. The horse-drawn carriage on the left in this 1905 card is their delivery van.

In 1912 Ellis Mills offered the latest in Ready to Hang lace curtains.

An Ellis Mills advertising card features the latest in millinery, probably from the 1950s.

Shaner and Romich Dry Goods Store stood on the northwest corner of High and Penn Streets. This is how it appeared before 1907.

Bressler's always carried the finest of men's apparel. This card is from 1965.

Yuletide trimmings are present in this postcard that the Shaner & Romich Dry Goods Store offered to its customers. This was after 1907, but certainly early in the century judging by clothing and fixtures.

This card from circa 1908 shows the whole north block of High Street from Penn to Hanover.

Mr. Bernhart certainly had a lovely office for his business on High Street, seen here in 1906.

Again, the north side of High Street between Charlotte and Penn Streets is pictured. Lamb's Music Store, a long time fixture in Pottstown at various locations, is to the right.

It is believed that this advertisement card with an address of North Hanover precedes the Lamb Store on High Street.

This card shows a better view of the auditorium building. The Bahr Arcade housed many businesses and professional people during its time. Before Sunnybrook, it was a venue for poultry shows and the like. Later it housed the farmer's market for many years. Some will remember it for the delicatessen, the stationary store, beautician salon, dentist, and doctors' offices. Also viewed is The Ledger building, which housed one of Pottstown's earlier newspapers. Later it became the home of Pep Boys and it is now the site of a floral shop.

This card captures the view of High Street looking west from Charlotte Street. The Bahr Arcade, now a parking lot, is on the left. The northwest corner, now a furniture store, houses a drug store in this early card, which also shows the addition of the trolley line to High Street. That northwest corner was also home to the YMCA and the Elks before those organizations acquired other accommodations.

Mr. Trout had several shops at different locations on High Street. This patriotically themed advertising card shows the vote for president in 1884 with both popular and electoral votes on the reverse.

This is a great view of the businesses on the north side of High Street between Hanover and Penn in the 1920s judging from all the Model T Fords. Please note diagonal parking heading in, making it much easier to negotiate than backing in as it is now. Also pictured is the National Iron Bank that, despite façade and name changes, remained a bank until recently.

This is a linen type card showing High Street as it appeared in the late 1930s. Although it is a very common card to find, it serves here to show the facades of the many stores.

Here we see Jack's Ambulance Service and some fire vehicles in front of the north side of High Street.

It appears that a very devastating fire consumed the Newberry's Store on High Street. It is believed this occurred about the middle of the twentieth century. One wonders how they were able to save the stores on either side with such a conflagration.

The Strand Theater captivates our attention here. Its original deco styling is very evident. It makes one wonder how anyone knew what film was playing with no marquee advertising.

Seen in the 1960s in this great chrome postcard done by Gene Orlando, the stores have changed a great deal in the span of about forty years. Newberry's has a new building, which in the twenty-first century is a cultural arts center.

"The Judge Steps Out" playing at the Strand Theater dates this card to 1949. See how much the theater has modernized. Block's Furniture now has taken the northwest corner of High and Charlotte Streets.

Mr. Hatfield wished all his customers a Happy New Year in 1875 and listed all his various products.

Before the Strand Theater, Edleman's sold shoes and trunks on the corner of High and Charlotte Streets.

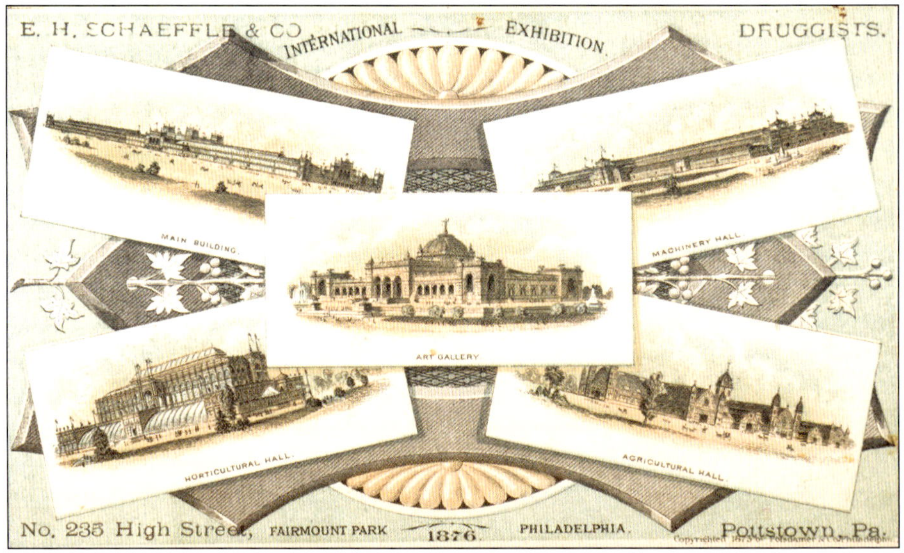

The druggists E. H. Schaeffle & Co. proved to be very cosmopolitan in offering this advertising card of the 1876 Centennial Exposition in Philadelphia. Although his name appears on the front, six other Pottstown merchants featured ads on the reverse.

At 267 High Street, prior to 1907, there was Becker's Barber Shop. Things of note on this postcard are the gas lighting fixtures and the shelves of individual shaving mugs.

Located at 221 High Street, I. G. Romich purveyed fine boots and shoes in the late 1800s.

Quicksell's, another Pottstown business, offers a restaurant in the rear and what appear to be candies in the front. Presentation of these candies is so elegant that, at first glance, it was believed to be the display of a jeweler or a pawnshop.

In the same time frame, at 246-248 High Street, Mr. Kulp sold hardware, agricultural equipment, and coal.

Very close to the Bahr Arcade, at 256 High Street, Dives, Pomeroy and Stewart had their department store. This was a forerunner of the later Pomeroy's stores, a chain in southeastern Pennsylvania.

Before 1907 these lovely shoes, advertised on this postcard, could be found at 257 High Street. This location remained in the shoe industry for many years.

Across the street from the St. Clair House at 211 High Street, Mr. Auchy engaged in the clothing business in the later nineteenth century.

This is a mechanical advertising card for Markley's Ice Cream that dates from the 1920s. No wonder her dress is so voluminous. She would walk a mile every day for a dish of ice cream! The walk evidently was not enough to burn the calories from the ice cream.

In 1886 Mr. Missimer offered a positive cure for dyspepsia (indigestion) and malaria, once not uncommon in our area.

1924 is the date of this ink blotter from Levin's Boot Shop at 232A High Street.

George Schwab featured fine confections at his store at 266-268 High Street.

"Get your picture done at Strunk's" at 254 High Street, this card from the late nineteenth century advertises.

In 1906 the Citizens Bank, built in 1894 and located at the northeast corner of High and Franklin Streets, resembled a church.

This is the new Citizen's Bank building erected in 1915. A portion of the Casselberry home, later to become the library, shows to the right of the card.

Farther east on the north side of High Street, Geist and March sold Prizer stoves. This attractive card was a reminder to shop there.

Now the site of a high rise for the elderly, this corner at High and Washington Streets is shown in the early twentieth century as the home of Porter's Drug Store.

This is a nice hand-colored card from the Keim Floral Co.

The Keim Shop changed hands when Oliver Christman bought the establishment. This beautifully colored chrome reveals the Christman floral and antiques shop when it was at its best. The Pottstown Historical Society now uses the building as their home.

Mr. Keim's business lasted many years. His 1909 calendar ad card must have been a delight to receive.

This is a pre 1906 view of the building housing the Meyerhoff Shirt Factory. The shell of the building still stands in the area of redevelopment near the Industrial Highway.

WILKE BUILDING. STORAGE HOUSE AND CABINET MAKER, POTTSTOWN, PA.

The Wilke Storage House and Cabinet Shop, located on Queen Street, is shown here in the early twentieth century. Begun in 1898, the shop remained as shown until 1936 when a tornado ripped through Pottstown and tore off the roof.

Latshaw's Grocery at the northeast corner of Charlotte and Oak Streets is now a residence. This early card represents the store at its peak. It remained open in the 1940s and young children went there for penny candy.

Wilke's Furniture House is pictured here in more recent times with an up-dated showroom. After the tornado, the company produced and refinished furniture.

The delivery wagon for Child's Cash Grocery is shown here circa 1907.

S. B. Wetherhold sold liquor from his store on King Street. This mechanical card, when closed, shows nice lace curtains, perhaps from Ellis Mills. When the tab is pulled, we see the couple engaged in a very passionate kiss.

Tommy Reidenouer sold stoves made by March Brownback at his store on King Street. Now replaced by an apartment building, the Reidenouer store for many years sold tin wares, such as stovepipe and rain gutters.

Minter's supplied the area's tombstones for many years. Located on North Hanover Street, it has been gone for a long time.

H. V. Smith's Grocery stood at the corner of High and Eden Streets.

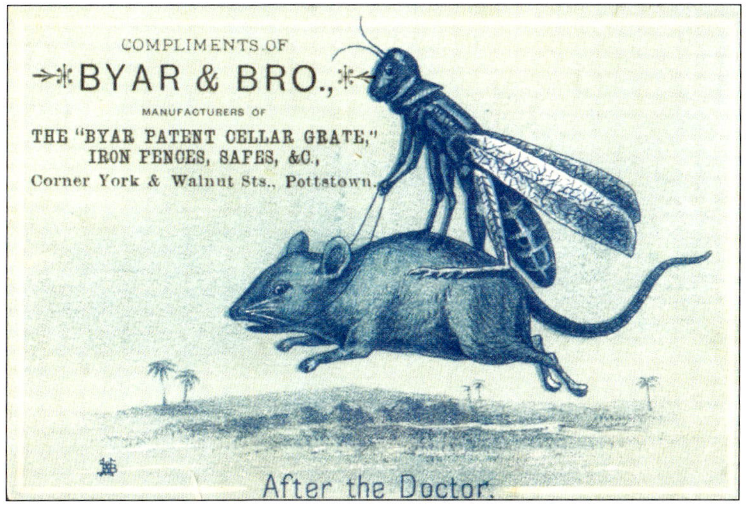

In the late 1900s Byar & Bro., located at the corner of York and Walnut Streets, sold iron fences, grates, and safes.

Burdan's Ice Cream became one of Pottstown's best known products in the early twentieth century. It had its beginnings in 1900 with an early venture called the "Dew Drop." Outgrowing their first plant at Beech and York Streets by 1913, a second plant at Manatawny and Second Streets was constructed. Harry Burdan died in 1924 and C. C., Harry's brother, sold interest in the company to the Philadelphia Dairy Products Company. The Pottstown operation produced condensed milk for the parent company for another half century.

It was easy to find Mr. Binder, the piano tuner, on Chestnut Street when you had this advertising card.

C. C. Burdan sent this Christmas card to customers in the 1920s.

Prince's Bakery, on South Washington Street, produced delicious bread with the most marvelous aroma. To pick up a warm loaf for Sunday sandwiches was a delightful experience. The small grocery store connected with the bakery is a spot well remembered by the older community.

Frederick Schwab had his bakery at 70 Charlotte Street in the late nineteenth century.

This grocery store stood at Third and York Streets. This is a very early photo, before the paving of York Street.

As It Started

On June 17, 1902, there was great activity in a little carpenter shop on Walnut Street. The first Schulz bread was coming out of the ovens—144 loaves which Mrs. Schulz herself had helped to bake. Her husband, Mr. John L. Schulz, and Mr. George Russell, now Treasurer of the Company, went out on foot, with baskets over their arms, and sold that bread from house to house.

Schulz Bakery began in 1902 as a cottage industry on Walnut Street, with Mrs. Schulz baking bread and her husband and one employee selling it door to door. This idea of sliced bread brought right to your home caught on. Perhaps they were the forerunner of the expression — "the greatest thing since sliced bread."

When in Season
They Sure Please 'Em

Scalloped Oysters

3 Tb. butter	Salt
$1\frac{1}{2}$ c. bread crumbs	Pepper
1 pt. oysters	$1\frac{1}{4}$ c. milk

Melt the butter, and pour over the bread crumbs. Use one-fourth of them to cover the bottom of a greased baking dish, cover with a layer of oysters, thoroughly cleaned and drained, season with salt and pepper, and add one-fourth more of the crumbs. Repeat until all are used, having crumbs on top. Add the strained liquid from the oysters and the milk. Bake at 400° F. until thoroughly done and brown.

Use SCHULZ BREAD

Schulz Bread continued delivery right to your door, using the familiar red and white trucks, for many years. A larger bakery on the Walnut Street site near The Hill School made this possible. Recipes to encourage the use of their bread were popular handouts.

Samples of Henricks' Pretzels were presented in waxed envelopes like this.

Long a staple business of Pottstown, Henricks' delivery van is shown at their location. It was near the old Pottstown Junior High School, now Pottstown Middle School, which can be seen in the background.

Apparently Mr. Shaner took these pictures of the Reliable Window Cleaners and their fleet to use as his marketing tools to sell other companies on the idea of photo advertising cards for their businesses.

People's Gas of Pottstown promised to save you money by using gas in 1908.

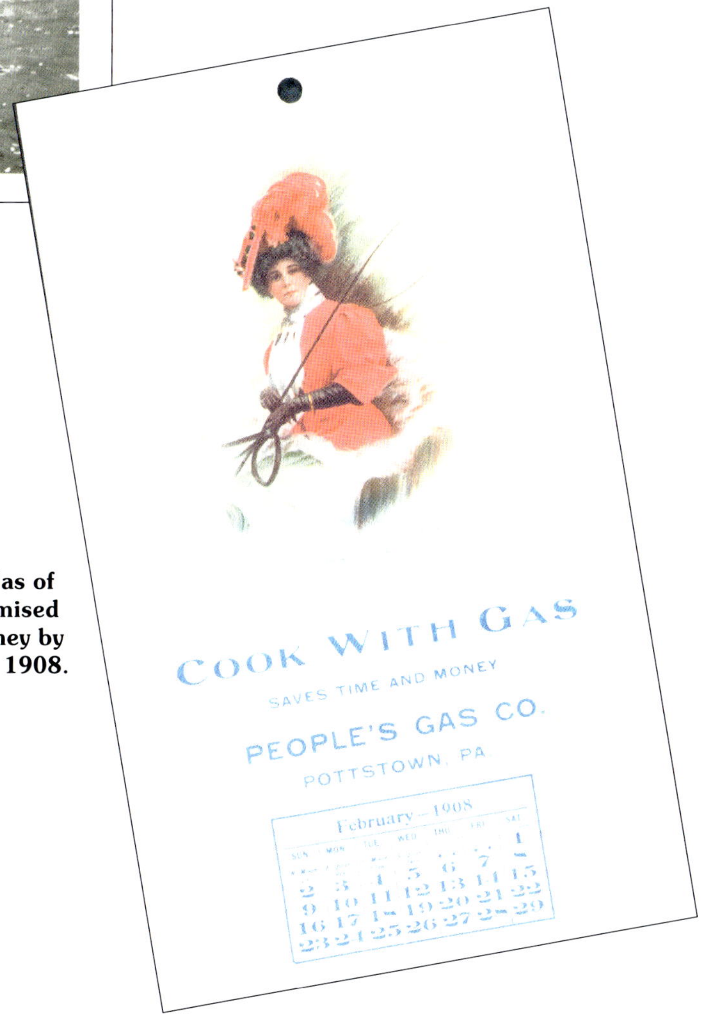

This 1910 Calendar advertising card from Bentz's Drug Store uses a beautiful woman to promote business.

This carriage maker operated on North Evans Street, just off High Street, before the turn of the twentieth century. The area is now a parking lot.

John Showalter hoped to win customers to purchase his Empire Washing Machines with the issuing of this dapper man on his advertising card at the turn of the nineteenth century. The improved Empire Washing Machine could be found at his establishment on the corner of Charlotte and Beech Streets.

PUBLIC SALE

OF

Western Penna. COWS

WILL BE SOLD AT PUBLIC SALE ON

THURSDAY, JUNE 25, '08

At Mansion House Stock Yards

M. E. Gilbert, Prop'r,

High and Keim Streets, Pottstown.

A Car Load Extra Fine Fresh Cows

This is a splendid lot of cows, consisting of DURHAMS, HOLSTEINS and full-blooded JERSEYS, and they will weigh from 1000 to 1200 pounds, are good baggers and milkers and can't be beat. Farmers and Dairymen in want of first-class stock do not miss this sale.

Also One Full-Blooded Stock Bull.

Sale rain or shine at 1.00 o'clock, P. M.

Conditions by

W. C. FORESMAN

J. P. Ecker, Auct.

W. H. Wagner, Clerk.

In 1908 the eastern end of Pottstown resembled the old west at the Mansion House Stock Yards. The Mansion House, a drover's hotel for many years, was the site of many cattle auctions and farm animal sales.

With the advent of mobile homes, a new business grew on High Street to accommodate them. Shaner's Mobile Home Park is still there.

In the Pottsgroves a number of orchards abounded. Fresh cider from fall apples is a taste treat.

Long an institution in Pottstown, *The Pottstown News* finally gave way to *The Pottstown Mercury*. This calendar from 1933 has on its reverse the numbers of the fire alarm boxes all over town. People were alerted to fire locations by the number of whistle toots that occurred.

Bause's Drug Store on North Charlotte Street came as a sister store to the one in Boyertown some time in the mid twentieth century. Eventually sold to Professional Pharmacy, the store continues to provide service to many people.

Jack's very clean and ornate gas station stood on West High Street on the north side just over the Manatawny Creek Bridge.

A Mutt and Jeff mechanical card advertises the Oakland and Pontiac cars sold at Kinsey-Golden Co. of 68 South Hanover Street.

Modern Motel of North Coventry, built and operated for many years by the Guest family, awaits the wreckers' ball at this time.

Another Gene Orlando card features a business across the street from the Modern Motel in the 1960s. A large shopping mall with a major anchor grocery has taken its place.

Laurel Locks Farms in North Coventry Township, shown here about 1940, have committed their farm acreage to land preservation making sure future generations will enjoy the view of unsullied farm land.

Just over the line from North Coventry, in East Coventry, the Peterman Veterinarian Hospital is shown here. Although it has changed hands, it remains an animal hospital to date.

For many years the Murphy Game Farm provided stock to the Pennsylvania Game Commission for the small game-hunting season. Hunting, for a fee, was done on this property as well.

Joe Davis sold this 1956 Mercury Montclair hardtop at his agency on High Street.

We sincerely hope that this book was a heavenly trip to Pottstown. A trip where, perhaps, old memories were stirred and relived or new information about the past was learned.

Kaiser and Frazer automobiles are pictured in 1949 at Bickel's Garage in Douglassville.

Bibliography

Chancellor, Paul and Marjorie Potts Wendell. *A History of Pottstown Pennsylvania*. Pottstown, Pennsylvania: The Feroe Press, 1953.

Cheadle, Dave. *Victorian Trade Cards*. Padukah, Kentucky: Collector Books, 1996.

Claussen, Edmunds W. *Journey through Our Land*. Pottstown, Pennsylvania: Mahr Printing Inc., 1970.

Cremers, Estelle. *Coventry, The Skool Kill District*. Morgantown, Pennsylvania: Masthof Press, 2003.

Davis, L. H. *Centennial Celebration at Pottstown, PA, July 4, 1876*. Pottstown, Pennsylvania: Centennial Committee, 1876.

Lichtenwalner, Muriel E. *Lower Pottsgrove Crossroads of History*. Lower Pottsgrove Township, Pennsylvania: Lower Pottsgrove Bicentennial Commission, 1979.

Mc Clintock, John. "Short History of the Postcard." *Antiques & Auction News*.

Smith, Patricia Wanger. *Around Pottstown*. Portsmouth, New Hampshire: Arcadia Publishing, 2004.

Southeastern Berks County. Portsmouth, New Hampshire: Arcadia Publishing, 2006.

Index

POTTSTOWN, PENNSYLVAN